# The Glass Pantry

old-fashioned preserving methods are well matched to today's life-style. Capturing the taste of spring-

time's tarragon or summer's basil in a flavored vinegar takes only long enough to put a handful of

the herbs into a glass jar, but throughout the year the homemade vinegar can be used in salads

or sauces as a reminder of those seasons. On a warm summer evening, pouring a small glass of

winter's vin d'orange or sipping the syrup of spring's brandied cherries is an elegant testimony to

one's own creativity and imagination, yet the initial preparation requires little more than putting the

fruit into wine or brandy months earlier.   ✦   To dry tomatoes, one needs to do no more than thinly

slice them and set them in the sun. Months later, as one reaches for the glass jar where the tomatoes

have been stored, the memories of summer come flooding back, to be savored again in deeply

rich sauces that nap pastas and cover pizzas. Dried apricots are created just as easily and are

intensely sweet and splendid enough to give as candy.   ✦   Part of the glass pantry resides in the

refrigerator. Relishes, chutneys, and confits of all kinds are stored there, ready to be taken out and

spread onto sandwiches or spooned into sauces. Another part of the glass pantry is the traditional pantry storage shelf, today most likely a spot in a cool basement or garage. There stand paraffin-sealed glass jars, glistening with a distinctive jelly, perhaps rose geranium or pomegranate, alongside jars of thick cherry preserves and a jar or two of tiny Zante grapes resting in amber Armagnac. Here, too, are the canned preserves of sunny yellow tomato ketchup and Italian pickled beets, of apricots in Marsala, Italian roasted peppers, and herb-laced figs. ◆ Winter's sugared nuts and spring's candied rose petals need no special storage conditions. They are kept in the part of the glass pantry on display on the kitchen counter or living room table where they can be admired—and eaten—by everyone. ◆ I have strong memories of a certain cut-glass dish with a round, fitted lid and a prism knob that my grandmother used for the candied walnuts and grapefruit peels she made at Christmas time. We lived in southern California, in what was then a small beach town, and my grandmother lived inland, fifty miles distant. When she came to visit us, she always brought shopping bags heavy with mason jars filled with peaches, pears, plums, apricots, and green beans, each bearing stickers carefully labeled in script with the date of canning—month and year—and

### BRANDIED FRUITS

Whole fruits or pieces of fruit can be preserved in alcohol, an environment in which microbes cannot live. The fruit is simply immersed in distilled spirits of 80 proof (40 percent alcohol), such as brandy, Cognac, eau-de-vie, gin, or vodka. Often a little sugar is added, as well. This is done either by putting sugar into the jar along with the fruit and allowing it to dissolve, or by first making a syrup with the sugar and a little of the alcohol. The covered jars are stored in a cool, dark place.

Brandied fruits will keep for a year or longer. No special equipment is required for making them.

### FRUITS IN SYRUP

Whole or sliced fruits—generally firm fruits that will retain their shape—are cooked in a light, medium, or heavy syrup. Juice, wine, herbs, or spices are sometimes added, as well. The cooked fruit will keep refrigerated for several days, but for long-term storage the fruit must be processed in a hot-water bath.

### INFUSED WINES

Simple flavored wines are made by adding fruits, herbs, or spices to red, white, or rosé wines. Sugar and distilled spirits are added as well, and the wine is put in a cool, dark place for twenty-four hours to thirty days. It is then strained and rebottled.

Infused wines will keep for up to one year when stored in a cool, dark place. No special equipment is needed for making infused wines other than wine bottles and corks.

### INFUSED VINEGARS

Vinegar is flavored in much the same way wine is. Fruits, herbs, or spices are added to vinegar of any kind. The vinegar is then put in a sunny spot or other warm location until it becomes sufficiently flavored, generally about ten days. The vinegar is strained, rebottled, and stored in a cool, dark place.

Infused vinegars will keep for six months or longer. No special equipment is needed for making flavored vinegars.

### INFUSED OILS

As with flavored wines and vinegars, fruits, herbs, or spices are put into oil and left there until the oil has become sufficiently infused with their flavor. The oil is then strained, rebottled, and stored in a cool, dark place.

These infused oils will keep for six months or longer. No special equipment is needed for making them.

### VEGETABLE CONFITS

Thin slices or pieces of vegetables are cooked slowly in fat, commonly olive oil or butter, but occasionally lard or other animal fats, along with a little sugar, salt, and sometimes herbs, until the vegetables virtually dissolve and caramelize somewhat. Confits will keep in tightly capped containers in a refrigerator for a week or more.

### PICKLES

Pickles are fruits or vegetables, either whole or in pieces, that have absorbed enough acid, most commonly the acetic acid in vinegar, to slow down microbial activity. To do this, however, the vinegar must be of at least 4 percent strength. Do not use homemade vinegar, as its strength cannot be accurately determined. Salt, spices, herbs, and sometimes sugar are added to the vinegar. Brines composed of salt and water are used to make fermented pickles, which are outside the scope of this book. Ketchups belong to the pickle category, as do relishes. In general, no special equipment is needed for pickle making.

Although pickles will keep refrigerated or in other cold-storage conditions for a short time, for long-term storage, pickles must be processed in a hot-water bath.

# Whole Cherry Preserves

CHERRIES ARE NATURALLY LOW IN PECTIN. IN ORDER FOR THEM TO JELL WHEN COOKED WITH ONLY SUGAR OR HONEY, THEY MUST BE SIMMERED LONG AND SLOWLY OVER VERY LOW HEAT, IN THE MANNER THAT CHERRY PRESERVES ARE STILL TRADITIONALLY MADE IN THE FRENCH AND GERMAN COUNTRYSIDES. DURING COOKING, THE CHERRIES BECOME PROFOUNDLY SWEET AND CHEWY, AND EVERY SPOONFUL TASTES LIKE FRUIT AND SUN REDUCED TO A SINGLE FLAVOR.

◆

*2 pounds ripe sweet cherries*
*such as Bing or Lambert*
*3¹/₂ cups granulated sugar*
*2 cups water*
*1 star anise*
*2 tablespoons honey*

◆

Discard any blemished cherries. Remove and discard the stems from the cherries. Pit them by gently squeezing each fruit until the pit pops out, leaving the cherry whole. If the pit does not pop out easily, slit the cherry open with a knife and pick out the pit. A cherry pitter may also be used, but it mangles the cherries more than the hand method does, and I find that it takes me only about 15 minutes to pit 2 pounds of cherries using the hand method. Set the pitted cherries aside.

Put the sugar and water in a large, heavy-bottomed stainless-steel or other nonreactive pot. Let stand, stirring occasionally, until the sugar dissolves, 5 or 10 minutes. Add the star anise and simmer over low heat, stirring from time to time, for 15 minutes. Remove the star anise and stir in the pitted cherries and the honey. Raise the heat and bring to a boil. Then again reduce the heat to low and simmer for about 1¾ hours, increasing the heat to medium-low after about 1½ hours. Be careful the preserves do not scorch.

After the first 45 minutes of cooking, begin to test for the jell point (see instructions on page 22). Alternatively, insert a candy thermometer in the mixture. When it reads 220 degrees F, the preserves are ready.

Remove from the heat. Skim off and discard any surface foam. Ladle the preserves into hot, dry, sterilized jars, filling to within ½ inch of the rims. Seal with a ⅛-inch-thick layer of melted paraffin (see directions for working with paraffin on page 22). Allow that layer to harden, then add a second layer of the same thickness. Using a damp cloth, wipe the rims clean. Cover with lids, aluminum foil, or with waxed paper or cotton cloth tightly fastened with twine or a rubber band.

Store in a cool, dark place. The preserves will keep for up to 1 year.

Makes about 4 pints

## Wild Greens and Garlic Relish

*N*O MATTER WHERE YOU LIVE,
SPRING WILL BRING A PROFUSION OF WILD
GREENS. FOR CENTURIES, THE FIRST GREENS
WERE THE SIGNAL THAT THE THRALL OF WINTER
HAD ENDED AND THAT SPRING, SUMMER, AND
FALL WOULD HOLD COURT ONCE MORE. THE
KNOWLEDGE OF WHICH GREENS WERE EDIBLE AND
WHICH WERE NOT HAS BEEN PASSED FROM
GENERATION TO GENERATION, AND EVEN TODAY
IN EUROPE ONE CAN SEE PEOPLE OF ALL AGES
OUT WITH GATHERING BASKETS, SEARCHING
ALONG ROADSIDES AND THE EDGES OF CULTI-
VATED FIELDS FOR SUCH DELICACIES AS YOUNG
PURSLANE, CHICORY, DANDELION, MUSTARD,
AND CRESS.

HERE, THE GREENS ARE MADE INTO A
RELISH—MORE A PURÉE THAN A TYPICAL
CHOPPED RELISH—THAT IS A GOOD ACCOMPANI-
MENT TO POACHED TROUT OR SALMON. I LIKE TO
STIR A TEASPOONFUL INTO A VINAIGRETTE
DRESSING, TOO.

to salads of all kinds. ✦ Summer's garden is full of pungent purple and green basil plants, so I continuously infuse vinegar with their harvest. I use the vinegar regularly for deglazing skillets of onion confit or caramelized sweet potatoes because of the unusual perfume summer's basil imparts to the finished dish. Wrapped with exotic ribbons and papers, the flavored vinegars make special gifts anytime of the year. ✦ For me, the most exotic of all summer's special preserves is rose geranium jelly. I put up only a few jars—I don't want to decimate my beautiful rose geranium plant—and only very reluctantly put the finished jars away in the basement, preferring to look at the light shining through the pale jelly sitting on my windowsill. ✦ Generally, I would rather eat summer's ripe fruits fresh from the trees and vines than to preserve them, but there are a few exceptions. Plum jam practically makes itself, which puts it high on my list of summer cooking, while a few jars of watermelon rind preserves are needed throughout the year for eating with curries and other spicy dishes. ✦ Summer preserving, like fall preserving, is highly personal because there is so much from which to choose. No single fruit or vegetable dominates the summer season as cherries and apricots do the spring or citrus fruits do the winter.

# Plum Jam

ONE OF THE MOST REWARDING OF ALL JAMS, PLUM JAM IS EASY TO PREPARE, COLORFUL, AND HAS A SATISFYING TASTE. SWEET, OF COURSE, BUT RETAINING ITS TART INTEGRITY NEVERTHELESS, PLUM JAM CAN BE MADE IN AT LEAST A HALF-DOZEN DIFFERENT COLORS, EACH ONE WITH A DISTINCTIVE FLAVOR. TINY WILD PLUMS MAKE A PALE PINK OR DELICATE YELLOW JAM, DEPENDING UPON WHICH KIND YOU USE, AND THE STURDY ELEPHANT HEART VARIETY YIELDS JARS OF DEEP RED. THE DIFFICULT-TO-FIND BLUE DAMSON PLUM, CONSIDERED BY MANY TO MAKE THE FINEST OF ALL PLUM JAMS, TURNS A REGAL PURPLE WHEN IT IS COOKED.

◆

*2¹/₂ pounds firm,*
*slightly underripe plums*
*3¹/₂ cups granulated sugar*

◆

Pit the plums, then chop them into fine bits to measure approximately 4 cups. Put the chopped fruit into a large, stainless-steel or other non-reactive saucepan and stir in the sugar. Let the mixture stand for 1 hour or so.

Over medium heat, bring the mixture slowly to a boil, stirring often. Cook rapidly, stirring often, for about 15 minutes, then begin to test for the jell point (see instructions on page 22). Alternatively, insert a candy thermometer in the mixture. When it reads 220 degrees F, the jam is ready.

Remove from the heat. Skim off and discard any surface foam. Ladle the jam into hot, dry, sterilized jars, filling to within ¼ inch of the rim. Seal with a ⅛-inch-thick layer of melted paraffin (see directions for working with paraffin on page 22).

Allow that layer to harden, then add a second layer of the same thickness. Using a damp cloth, wipe the rims clean. Cover with lids, aluminum foil, or with waxed paper or cotton cloth tightly fastened with twine or a rubber band.

Store in a cool, dark place. The jam will keep for up to 1 year.

Makes about 2 pints

*Rose Geranium Jelly*

ALF THE PLEASURE OF MAKING

THIS JELLY IS THE FUN OF USING AN INGREDIENT

AS EXOTIC AS SCENTED GERANIUM LEAVES.

PLUCKING THE INTENSELY PERFUMED LEAVES

FROM THE DECORATIVE POTTED PLANT THAT SITS

IN MY DINING ROOM WINDOW, THEN PACKING THEM

INTO AN ORDINARY MEASURING CUP SEEMS STEPS

REMOVED FROM THE PRACTICAL PROCESS OF

TURNING FRUITS INTO JELLY AND MORE AKIN TO A

CHILD'S GAME OF MAKING SECRET POTIONS. THE

INFUSION MADE FROM STEEPING THE LEAVES

IMPARTS A LINGERING, SLIGHTLY MYSTERIOUS

FLAVOR THAT BECOMES DISCERNIBLE A MOMENT

AFTER SWALLOWING—MUCH LIKE A SURPRISING

FINISH ON A MEMORABLE WINE.

THE UNRIPE APPLES PROVIDE NATURAL

PECTIN FOR THE JELLING, BUT CONTRIBUTE SUR-

PRISINGLY LITTLE TO THE TASTE. IF YOU CANNOT

FIND UNRIPE GREEN APPLES, SUBSTITUTE TART

GREEN COOKING APPLES.

Peel the skin from the rind and scrape the rind clean of any flesh. Cut the rind into ½-inch cubes. Combine 4 quarts of the water and the salt in a large bowl and stir to dissolve the salt. Add the rind and let soak overnight at room temperature.

The next day, drain the rind. Place it in a stainless-steel or other nonreactive saucepan with 2 cups of the remaining water and bring to a boil over high heat. Lower the heat and simmer until the rind is just tender when pierced with a fork, about 50 minutes. Drain well and set aside.

In a saucepan large enough to hold the rind eventually, combine all the remaining ingredients, including the remaining 2 cups water. Bring slowly to a boil, stirring to dissolve the sugar. Boil until the sugar dissolves and a syrup forms, about 5 minutes. Add the rind and cook over low heat until it becomes transparent, about 30 minutes.

Using a slotted utensil, remove the rind pieces and pack them tightly into hot, clean, dry jars with sealable lids. Ladle the hot syrup into the jars, filling the jars to within ½ inch of the rims. Using a damp cloth, wipe the rims clean. Cover with the lids and process for 30 minutes in a hot-water bath (see instructions for processing hot-pack foods on page 21).

Remove the jars and let them cool 12 hours or overnight. Check for a complete seal.

Store the sealed jars in a cool, dark place. The preserves will keep for up to 1 year. Once opened, keep refrigerated. Store any jar lacking a good seal in the refrigerator for up to 2 weeks.

Makes 2 to 3 pints

## Fresh Herb and Vegetable Relish

*T*HIS IS ONE OF THE MOST FLAVORFUL RELISHES I KNOW. THE DISTINCTIVE TASTES
OF THE FRESH HERBS INTERMINGLE AND BLEND WITH THOSE OF THE CRUNCHY, FINELY DICED
VEGETABLES, AS ALL OF THE INGREDIENTS STEEP TOGETHER IN THE BRINE. A VERSATILE
RELISH, IT MAY BE SPREAD ON SANDWICHES OR SERVED AS A SPICY SIDE DISH TO CLASSICALLY
SIMPLE MEAT DISHES SUCH AS ITALIAN *bollito misto*.

◆

*1/4 cup finely diced cabbage*
*2 cups finely diced,*
*peeled cucumber*
*1 cup finely diced onion*
*1 1/2 cups finely diced fennel*
*1/4 cup finely diced garlic*
*1 cup finely diced red*
*or green sweet pepper*
*1 cup finely diced celery*
*1 1/4 cups finely minced*
*mixed fresh parsley, mint,*
*tarragon, basil, and chives,*
*in any ratio*
*2 tablespoons salt*
*6 cups red wine vinegar*

◆

Combine all of the ingredients in a large glass bowl. Cover and refrigerate for 4 days.

Using a slotted utensil, remove the vegetables from the bowl, reserving the vinegar, and snugly pack them into dry, sterilized jars with lids to within ½ inch of the rims. Pour in enough of the vinegar to cover the vegetables completely. Cover with the lids.

The relish will keep in the refrigerator for up to 3 months.

Makes about 3 pints

# Yellow Tomato Ketchup

THIS SPICY TOMATO KETCHUP CAN BE SERVED IN MUCH THE SAME WAY AS APPLESAUCE—CHILLED OR AT ROOM TEMPERATURE AS AN ACCOMPANIMENT TO VEGETABLES, SUCH AS CRISPY POTATO PANCAKES, OR WITH OMELETS, FRITTATAS, SOUFFLÉS, PORK CHOPS, SAUSAGES, FISH, OR CHICKEN. ITS THICK, FAINTLY CHUNKY TEXTURE HAS APPLESAUCE'S FAMILIAR HINTS OF CLOVE, CINNAMON, AND LEMON, PLUS THE EXOTIC OVERTONES OF CORIANDER, GINGER, GARLIC, AND SWEET PEPPERS.

◆

10 large, very ripe yellow tomatoes
(about 5 pounds)

2 large yellow sweet peppers,
seeded, deribbed, and coarsely
chopped (about 1 1/2 pounds)

2 onions (about 3/4 pound)

10 cloves garlic

1 cup white wine vinegar

Juice and grated zest of 1/4 lemon

3/4 cup granulated sugar

1 1/2 teaspoons salt

2 teaspoons mustard seeds

1 tablespoon black peppercorns

1 tablespoon coriander seeds

1 teaspoon whole cloves

1 cinnamon stick,
about 1 inch long

1-inch-piece fresh ginger,
cut into 3 or 4 pieces

◆

Bring a large saucepan filled with water to a boil. Immerse the tomatoes in the boiling water for 30 seconds. Lift out the tomatoes with a slotted utensil and, when cool enough to handle, peel off the skins. Cut in half crosswise and squeeze gently to remove the seeds, using your fingertip to dislodge any that do not fall out easily.

Put the tomatoes, sweet peppers, onions, garlic, 1/2 cup of the vinegar, and the lemon zest and juice in a stainless-steel or other nonreactive saucepan large enough to hold all the ingredients eventually. Cook over medium heat, stirring frequently, until the vegetables are soft and cooked through, 15 to 20 minutes.

Transfer the vegetable mixture to a blender or to a food processor fitted with the steel blade. Process until coarsely puréed but not liquefied. Return the purée to the pan, and add the sugar, salt, and the remaining 1/2 cup vinegar.

Cut out an 8-inch square of cheesecloth. Place in the center the mustard seeds, peppercorns, coriander seeds, cloves, cinnamon stick, and ginger. Gather up the corners and tie them with kitchen string to make a spice bag. Add to the pan holding the purée.

Bring the vegetable mixture to a simmer over low heat and continue to simmer, stirring occasionally, until it thickens, about 1 hour. Watch carefully so it does not burn. The finished ketchup will be slightly thinner than most commercial ketchups.

Ladle the hot ketchup into clean, dry jars with sealable lids, filling the jars to within 1/2-inch of the rims. Using a damp cloth, wipe the rims clean. Cover with the lids and process for 30 minutes in a hot-water bath (see instructions for processing hot-pack foods on page 21).

Remove the jars and let them cool 12 hours or overnight. Check the lids for a complete seal. Store the sealed jars in a cool, dark place. The ketchup will keep for up to 1 year. Once opened, keep refrigerated. Store any jar lacking a good seal in the refrigerator for up to 10 days.

Makes about 2 quarts

# Green or Purple Basil Vinegars

SOME TIME AGO I STOOD IN FRONT OF AN ARRAY OF EXQUISITE, JEWEL-TONED VINEGARS AT THE FAMED FAUCHON IN PARIS. SMALL, ELEGANT, AND EXPENSIVE BOTTLES OF VINAIGRE DE CASSIS, DE FRAISE, DE MYRTILLE, DE CERISE TOOK UP AN ENTIRE SHELF. I BOUGHT A BOTTLE OF DEEP PURPLE VINAIGRE DE CASSIS AND CAREFULLY PACKED IT IN MY CARRY-ON BAG. I USED IT ONLY ON SPECIAL OCCASIONS, AND THEN AS SPARINGLY AS POSSIBLE, BECAUSE I WANTED IT TO LAST FOREVER.

SINCE THEN, I HAVE DISCOVERED THAT HERB- AND FRUIT-INFUSED VINEGARS ARE QUITE SIMPLE TO MAKE. THE FLAVOR OF BASIL VINEGAR—OR ANY OTHER INFUSED VINEGAR—WILL VARY DEPENDING UPON THE STRENGTH AND VARIETY OF THE VINEGAR USED, AS WELL AS THE AMOUNT AND THE VARIETY OF FLAVORING. THE PURPLE BASIL PRODUCES A MAGNIFICENT DEEP BURGUNDY VINEGAR, A VISUAL TREAT, WITH A FINE, SLIGHTLY HOT BASIL TASTE. GREEN BASIL, ON THE OTHER HAND, COLORS THE VINEGAR TO A FAINT GREEN, AND THE RESULTING TASTE IS PURE BASIL, WITHOUT THE HINT OF HEAT FOUND IN THE PURPLE VARIETY.

◆

*1 cup loosely packed green*
*or purple basil sprigs*
*3¹/₂ cups distilled white wine vinegar*

◆

Gently crush the basil between your fingertips, just enough to begin releasing the volatile oils. Put the basil into a dry, sterilized jar with a lid. Pour in the vinegar and cover with the lid. Place the jar in a sunny location, indoors or outside, and let stand about 10 days, or until the vinegar has become infused with the flavor of the basil to your satisfaction.

Strain the vinegar through a sieve lined with several layers of cheesecloth; discard the basil. Decant into dry, sterilized bottles. Seal with corks and store the bottles in a cool, dark place. The vinegar will keep for up to 1 year.

Makes about 1½ pints

## Lavender Syrup

*L*AVENDER IS GENERALLY THOUGHT OF IN A FLORAL RATHER THAN A CULINARY SENSE, BUT IT HAS A LONG HISTORY OF BEING USED TO MAKE HOT, TEALIKE INFUSIONS AND TO FLAVOR SUCH SWEETS AND BAKED GOODS AS ICE CREAMS, CUSTARDS, BREADS, AND COOKIES. THIS SYRUP IS DELICATELY SCENTED, SWEET, AND LIGHT, WITH ONLY THE FAINTEST TASTE OF THE FLOWER'S HEAVENLY PERFUME. IT GIVES EXOTIC FLAIR TO FRUIT SALADS, AND A DROP OR TWO IN A GLASS OF CHAMPAGNE MAKES AN ELEGANT APERITIF.

◆

*4 cups water*

*2 cups granulated sugar*

*$1/2$ cup pesticide-free fresh lavender flowers, or 2 tablespoons dried lavender flowers*

◆

Combine the water and sugar in a stainless-steel or other nonreactive saucepan and bring to a boil over high heat, stirring. Reduce the heat to medium and simmer, continuing to stir, until the sugar dissolves and a thin syrup forms, about 10 minutes. Remove from the heat, add the lavender blossoms, cover, and let stand overnight in a cool place.

The next day, strain the syrup through a sieve lined with several layers of cheesecloth; discard the blossoms. Decant into dry, sterilized bottles. Seal with corks and store the bottles in a cool, dark place. The syrup will keep for 3 months or more.

Makes about 2 pints

# Pears Pickled in Merlot

$O$F THE MANY PRESERVES MADE BY MY GRANDMOTHER, ONE OF THE FEW MADE ALSO BY MY MOTHER WAS PICKLED PEACHES. EVERY SUMMER MOTHER MADE TWO OR THREE LARGE JARS, AND WE GENERALLY ATE THEM DURING THE CHRISTMAS HOLIDAYS. WHEN I WAS FIRST MARRIED, I, TOO, PUT UP PICKLED PEACHES. THESE WINE-INFUSED PICKLED PEARS ARE A MORE ELEGANT PREPARATION, AND I THINK MORE VERSATILE.

THE PEARS, WITH THEIR HINT OF WINE, CINNAMON, AND ROSEMARY, GO EQUALLY WELL WITH ROASTED MEATS OR COOKED BEANS SUCH AS BLACK-EYED PEAS, OR THEY CAN BE SERVED FOR DESSERT, ALONE OR WITH ICE CREAM, CAKE, OR COOKIES.

◆

*10 firm pears*

*such as Red Bartlett or Bosc*

*(about 3¹/₂ pounds)*

*1 fifth Merlot*

*3 cups red wine vinegar*

*6 cups granulated sugar*

*1 tablespoon chopped*

*fresh rosemary*

*3 cinnamon sticks,*

*each about 4 inches long*

◆

Peel the pears, leaving the stems intact. Set aside.

Combine the wine, vinegar, sugar, rosemary, and cinnamon in a stainless-steel or other nonreactive pan large enough to hold all the whole pears eventually. Bring to a boil over high heat. Boil, stirring often, until a thin syrup forms, about 5 minutes. Using a slotted utensil, slip the pears into the boiling syrup. Reduce the heat to medium and gently boil the pears, turning them in the syrup, until just barely cooked, 8 to 10 minutes. Be careful not to overcook them to the point where they become mushy.

Using a slotted utensil, transfer the pears to clean, dry jars with sealable lids. To pack the pears, make a layer of pears, standing them upright, then add a second layer of pears, inverting them, to maximize the space. Ladle in the hot syrup, including the cinnamon sticks, to cover the pears completely and to fill the jars to within ½ inch of the rims. Using a damp cloth, wipe the rims clean. Cover with the lids and process for 1 hour in a hot-water bath (see instructions for processing hot-pack foods on page 21).

Remove the jars and let them cool for 12 hours or overnight. Check for complete seals.

Store the sealed jars in a cool, dark place. The pears will keep for up to 1 year. Once opened, keep refrigerated. Store any jar lacking a complete seal in the refrigerator for up to 10 days.

Makes 3 pints

*Figs Pickled in Balsamic Vinegar and
Herbes de Provence*

A FEW YEARS AGO I WAS IN THE BOULANGERIE OF A BACK-COUNTRY VILLAGE IN HAUTE-PROVENCE. ON DISPLAY IN ADDITION TO LOAVES OF BREAD, CROISSANTS, PAIN AU CHOCOLAT, AND THE USUAL BAKERY ASSORTMENT OF WRAPPED CANDIES AND HARD COOKIES, THERE STOOD A SHORT ROW OF GLASS JARS BANDED WITH HAND-PRINTED LABELS AND TOPPED WITH TWINE-TIED CAPS OF YELLOW-AND-RED PROVENÇAL CLOTH. A WHITE CARD SIGNALED FAIT Á LA MAISON—"HOMEMADE." ON CLOSER INSPECTION I SAW THE JARS CONTAINED FIGUES AUX HERBES DE PROVENCE. NATURALLY I BOUGHT ONE.

THE INTENSE SUGAR TYPICAL OF FALL FIGS WAS TEMPERED BY A SWEET-SOUR SYRUP, AND THROUGHOUT WAS THE SURPRISING PEPPERY, UNDERBRUSH TASTE OF THE WOODY THYME AND JUNIPER OF THE REGION'S BRUSH. EVEN THOUGH I INTENDED TO, I NEVER RETURNED TO THE BOULANGERIE TO TELL THE OWNERS HOW WON-DERFUL THE PICKLED FIGS WERE AND TO FIND OUT EXACTLY HOW THEY WERE MADE. ON RETURNING TO CALIFORNIA I PUT UP MY OWN VERSION, BASED ON MY MEMORY OF THE TASTE.

# Quince Slices in Vanilla Syrup

QUINCE IS AN EXCEPTIONAL FRUIT THAT WAS FAR MORE POPULAR AND AVAIL-ABLE IN THE PAST. BECAUSE OF THEIR HIGH-PECTIN CONTENT, QUINCES WERE FREQUENTLY COMBINED WITH LOW-PECTIN FRUITS AS WELL AS PREPARED ON THEIR OWN. ALTHOUGH INEDIBLE WHEN RAW, THEY TAKE ON A HONEYED SWEETNESS AKIN TO ASIAN PEARS WHEN COOKED IN A SYRUP, AS THEY ARE HERE.

THE FRUITS ALSO CHANGE THEIR COLOR WHEN COOKED, TURNING FROM PASTY WHITE TO A DEEP ROSE-AMBER. THESE VANILLA-INFUSED SLICES CAN BE EATEN AS A COMPOTE, WARM OR COLD. THEY MAY ALSO BE SERVED ON THEIR OWN AS A CONDIMENT TO ACCOMPANY ANY SAVORY DISH OR USED AS A PIE FILLING. I FIND THEM ESPECIALLY GOOD AT BREAKFAST, WHEN I LIKE TO SLIP A SPOONFUL OR TWO INTO WARM OATMEAL WITH A LITTLE CREAM.

◆

*6 quinces (about 3 pounds)*
*4 cups granulated sugar*
*4 cups water*
*1 vanilla bean,*
*about 8 inches long*
*2 tablespoons fresh lemon juice*

◆

Peel and core the quinces and carefully remove and discard the seeds. Cut the fruits lengthwise into slices ½ inch thick. Set aside.

Combine the sugar, water, vanilla bean, and lemon juice in a stain-less-steel or other non-reactive saucepan large enough to hold the quince eventually. Bring the mixture to a boil over medium-high heat and continue to boil, stirring often, until a light- to medium-thick syrup forms, about 10 minutes. Reduce the heat and add the quince slices. Poach the fruits until just barely tender when pierced with the tines of a fork, about 15 minutes. Cooking time will vary depending upon the maturity of the fruits.

Using a slotted utensil, tightly pack the quince slices into clean, dry jars with sealable lids. Ladle in the hot syrup to within ½ inch of the rims. Using a damp cloth, wipe the rims clean. Cover with the lids and process for 40 minutes in a hot-water bath (see instructions for processing hot-pack foods page 21).

Remove the jars and let them cool for at least 12 hours or overnight. Check the lids for a complete seal.

Store the sealed jars in a cool, dark place. The quince slices will keep for up to 1 year. Once opened, keep them refrigerated. Store any jar lacking a good seal in the refrigerator for up to 1 week.

Makes about 4 pints

# Zante Grapes in Armagnac

ZANTE GRAPES, GROWN PRIMARILY FOR DRYING TO BE SOLD AS CURRANTS, ARE RARELY LARGER THAN A SMALL PEA AND OFTEN THE SIZE OF A PLUMP PEPPERCORN. BECAUSE OF THEIR MINUSCULE SIZE AND TIGHTLY BUNCHED GROWTH HABIT, SWEET, BERRY-FLAVORED ZANTES ARE BEST EATEN BY THE CLUSTER RATHER THAN ONE BY ONE, AND THEY CAN BE PRESERVED IN CLUSTERS AS WELL.

ONLY A RELATIVELY SMALL AMOUNT OF ZANTE GRAPES REACH THE FRESH MARKET, APPEARING FOR A FEW WEEKS IN FALL. THEY ARE FREQUENTLY PROMOTED AS CHAMPAGNE GRAPES, THE MARKETING IDEA BEING TO DROP A FEW GRAPES INTO A GLASS OF CHAMPAGNE WHERE THE TINY, PALE ROSE SPHERES SEEM LIKE BUBBLES.

CERTAINLY THESE ARMAGNAC-PRESERVED ZANTE GRAPES MAY BE ADDED TO CHAMPAGNE, BUT LIKE JUDY ROGERS, THE CHEF AT SAN FRANCISCO'S ZUNI CAFE WHO GAVE ME THIS RECIPE, I PREFER TO PARTNER THE PICKLED GRAPES WITH SAVORY, STRONG-FLAVORED DISHES SUCH AS ROAST DUCK OR PHEASANT, ADDING THEM TO THE SAUCE CREATED FROM THE PAN JUICES.

◆

1$^1/_2$ pounds Zante grape bunches

$^2/_3$ cup granulated sugar

1$^1/_2$ cups Armagnac

or other brandy

◆

Separate the bunches
into clusters about 1
inch across, removing
and discarding any
damaged grapes. Put
the clusters into a dry,
sterilized widemouthed
jar with a lid. Sprinkle
the sugar over the grape
clusters and pour in
the Armagnac. Cover
with the lid.

Place in a cool, dark
place or in the refrigerator. Every day turn and
jostle the jar until the
sugar dissolves com-
pletely. This will take
about 10 days.

The grapes will be
ready in about 2 weeks,
but the flavor will mellow
over time. Store in a
cool, dark place. The
grapes will keep for up
to 1 year.

Makes about 1½ pints

# Salsa all'Agresto

Marco Fiorini, chef at San Francisco's elegant Blue Fox restaurant, told me of this traditional recipe. His family is from the Valtellina, a rugged, steeply narrow alpine valley northeast of Milan that climbs steadily from the far reaches of Lake Como to the Swiss border. Marco told me this sauce has been made in the region since the Middle Ages.

Used in place of vinegar, the juice of unripened grapes is the source of the sauce's tart, unusual taste, with bread, herbs, and almonds composing the balance. The sauce has a particular affinity for veal and trout, which is unsurprising when one considers that the Valtellina has both numerous dairies and many streams in the surrounding mountains.

◆

*1 large bunch unripened table or wine grapes such as Concord, Thompson seedless, or Cabernet Sauvignon (about 1 1/2 pounds)*

*1/2 cup fine fresh bread crumbs*

*1 teaspoon granulated sugar*

*2 tablespoons chopped fresh parsley*

*1/2 teaspoon salt*

*1/2 teaspoon freshly ground black pepper*

*2 garlic cloves*

*1/2 cup unsalted almonds*

*1/4 cup chicken stock, if serving sauce heated*

◆

Discard any grapes that are bruised or damaged. Crush the grapes, using a mortar and pestle, in a bowl with the back of a wooden spoon, or in a food mill. Strain the juice through a fine mesh sieve and discard the skins, seeds, and stems. You should have approximately 1 cup juice; set aside.

Combine the bread crumbs, sugar, parsley, salt, pepper, garlic, and almonds in a blender or a food processor fitted with the steel blade. Purée the mixture.

Slowly add the grape juice and process until a thick paste forms.

Spoon the paste into a dry, sterilized jar with a lid. Cover and refrigerate for up to 1 week.

The sauce may be used chilled, at room temperature, or heated. To use the sauce warm, place the chicken stock in a saucepan and stir in the sauce. Heat gently; do not let the mixture boil or the sauce will separate.

Makes about ¾ pint

# *Italian Wine Conserve*

*S*OMETIME AGO I VISITED A SEED COMPANY IN NORTHERN ITALY DURING THE GRAPE HARVEST AND WINE-MAKING SEASON. DRIVING ALONG THE NARROW COUNTRY ROADS WITH MY HOST, WE HAD TO MAKE WAY FOR HORSES AND TRACTORS PULLING WAGON LOADS OF GRAPES. THE YEASTY SMELL OF THE CRUSHED, FERMENTING FRUITS WAFTED ON THE AIR AS WE PASSED LARGE FARMHOUSES WHERE THE RESIDENTS MADE THEIR OWN WINE. AS WE WENDED OUR WAY ACROSS THE HILLS, MY HOST DESCRIBED THE CULINARY DELIGHTS OF THE AREA, INCLUDING A LOCAL CONSERVE TRADITIONALLY MADE ON THE SEVENTH DAY OF FERMENTATION.

AS I UNDERSTOOD IT, THE FROTH OF THE FERMENTING WINE IS SKIMMED, AND THE SKIMMINGS ARE THEN COMBINED WITH SUGAR AND COOKED INTO A THICK JAM TO WHICH SMALL PIECES OF DRIED APRICOTS, PEARS, AND WALNUTS ARE ADDED. UNFORTUNATELY, I NEVER GOT TO TRY IT, BUT I DEVISED THIS RECIPE BASED ON HOW I IMAGINED IT WOULD TASTE.

---

◆

*1 quince*

*1 bunch grapes,*

*preferably Concord, Zinfandel,*

*or another wine grape*

*(about 1¹/₂ pounds)*

*1 cup fruity wine*

*such as Gamay Beaujolais*

*2 cups granulated sugar*

*1 lemon zest strip,*

*about 1 inch long*

*¹/₂ cup chopped dried apricots*

*³/₄ cup chopped dried pears*

*1 cup chopped walnuts*

◆

---

Peel and core the quince and carefully remove and discard the seeds. Grate the quince and set aside. Discard any grapes that are bruised or damaged. Crush the grapes, using a mortar with a pestle, in a bowl with the back of a wooden spoon, or in a food mill. Strain the juice through a fine-mesh sieve and discard the skins, seeds, and stems. You should have approximately 1 cup juice; set aside.

Combine the grape juice, wine, sugar, quince, and lemon zest in a stainless-steel or other nonreactive sauce-pan. Bring to a boil over medium-high heat, stirring to dissolve the sugar. Continue to boil, stirring constantly, until the mixture thickens, about 15 minutes. Stir in the apricots and pears and cook for another 15 minutes. Stir in the walnuts. Remove from the heat.

Ladle the conserve into clean, dry jars with sealable lids, filling the jars to within a ½ inch of the rims. Using a damp cloth, wipe the rims clean. Cover with the lids and process for 40 minutes in a hot-water bath (see instructions for processing hot-pack foods on page 21).

Remove the jars and let them cool for 12 hours or overnight. Check for complete seals.

Store the sealed jars in a cool, dark place. The conserve will keep for up to 1 year. Once opened, keep them refrigerated. Store any jar lacking a good seal in the refrigerator for up to 2 weeks.

Makes 1½ pints

Preheat an oven to 350 degrees F.

Wash the leeks well to remove any gritty bits of sand and soil caught between the layers of leaves. Neatly trim off the fibrous roots and the uppermost dark green leaves and discard. Cut the leeks, both the white and green parts, into ¼-inch-thick slices.

Butter a shallow baking pan large enough to hold the sliced leeks in a layer 1 inch deep. Add the leeks, drizzle the olive oil on them, then sprinkle with salt and sugar.

Put the leeks in the preheated oven and roast, turning often, until they appear melted and are a creamy gold, 45 minutes to 1 hour.

Remove them from the oven and let cool to room temperature. Spoon the leeks into dry, sterilized jars with lids. Cover and store in the refrigerator. The leeks will keep for up to 2 weeks.

Makes about 2 pints

WHEN I WAS LIVING IN FRANCE, I MADE AND SOLD FRESH GOAT CHEESES. ONE OF MY FIRST CUSTOMERS WAS AN AUBERGE LOCATED NEXT TO AN OLD CHURCH IN A MEDIEVAL VILLAGE PRECARIOUSLY PERCHED ATOP A HILL. THE SETTING WAS FORMIDABLE, AS WAS THE COOK, WHO HAD A REPUTATION FOR BEING TEMPERAMENTAL, SO I ALWAYS MADE MY DELIVERIES WITH A LITTLE TREPIDATION. ONE DAY I FOUND THE COOK IN AN EXPANSIVE MOOD AND WAS INVITED IN. THE RED-TILED KITCHEN WAS FILLED WITH BASKETS OF FRUITS AND VEGETABLES FROM THE GARDEN; BUNCHES OF WILD HERBS FESTOONED THE OPEN FIREPLACE AND HAND-HEWN, DARK WOODEN WORK TABLES SAT SQUARELY IN THE CENTER. I WAS ENTRANCED.

THE COOK, WHOSE NAME I HAVE SINCE FORGOTTEN, TOOK ME OVER TO A SIDEBOARD AND SHOWED ME A LARGE GLASS JAR HALF FULL OF BITS AND CHUNKS OF GOAT CHEESE RESTING IN RICH GREEN OLIVE OIL FLAVORED WITH PEPPERCORNS AND HERBS. THE SUN, COMING THROUGH A PANED WINDOW, CAST THE EDGE OF THE JAR IN LIGHT, AND THE WHOLE ARRAY OF LIGHT AND RICH COLORS LOOKED LIKE AN ARTIST'S COMPOSITION. THE COOK EXPLAINED THAT HIS CUSTOMERS WERE PLEASED WITH MY FRESH CHEESE, SO TO PRESERVE ITS FRESHNESS AND PREVENT IT FROM DRYING OUT, HE ALWAYS PUT ANY LEFTOVER CHEESE INTO THE OLIVE OIL. THAT WAY, BETWEEN MY TWICE-WEEKLY DELIVERIES, HE WOULD ALWAYS HAVE "FRESH" CHEESE.

ONCE HOME, I TRIED IT WITH MY OWN CHEESE, AND ALTHOUGH IT WASN'T QUITE "FRESH" TO MY THINKING, I LOVED THE EXTRA TASTE AND RICHNESS IMPARTED BY THE SEASONED OIL. THEREAFTER, I KEPT A JAR OF CHEESE IN OLIVE OIL FOR THE BEAUTY OF IT, AS WELL AS FOR THE TASTE OF IT IN SALADS OR SIMPLY SPREAD ON A SLICE OF COUNTRY BREAD.

**B**OTTLES OF OLIVE OIL CONTAINING DRIED RED CHILIES, BLACK PEPPERCORNS, AND THE WILD HERBS OF THE REGION SIT ON THE TABLES OF EVERY PIZZERIA IN PROVENCE. WHEN A THIN, CRISP PIZZA IS SERVED DIRECTLY FROM THE WOOD-BURNING OVEN, THE FIRST THING TO DO IS TO SPRINKLE IT WITH SOME OF THE CHILI OIL.

THESE COLORFUL BOTTLES MAKE CHARMING GIFTS FOR PIZZA LOVERS, ESPECIALLY WHEN ACCOMPANIED WITH A PIZZA CUTTER, A BOUQUET OF DRIED HERBS, A SPECIAL CALABRIAN SAUSAGE, A BLOCK OF PARMIGIANO-REGGIANO, OR OTHER ACCOUTREMENTS ASSOCIATED WITH THE MAKING AND EATING OF PIZZA.

✦

*1 tablespoon black peppercorns*

*3 fresh or dried bay leaves*

*5 small dried hot red chili*

*peppers, with seeds intact*

*3 fresh thyme sprigs,*

*each 3 to 4 inches long*

*2 cups olive oil*

✦

In the order listed, put all of the ingredients into a dry, sterilized wine bottle. Seal with a cork and store in a cool, dark place for at least 2 or 3 weeks to allow time for the oil to become infused with the other flavors.

The oil will keep for several months. To make a sprinkler top, cut a ¼-inch-deep, V-shaped channel the length of the cork.

Makes 1 pint

*12 navel oranges*
*(about 4 1/2 pounds)*
*4 lemons (about 1 1/2 pounds)*
*2 quarts water*
*5 pounds granulated sugar*

Peel the oranges and lemons—zest only, no pith—as thinly as you can. Slice the peel from 1 orange into paper-thin strips about 1/16 inch wide. You will have about 1/4 cup. Put the remaining peels into a blender or a food processor fitted with the steel blade and chop.

Put the hand-sliced peel and the machine-chopped peel into a heavy-bottomed pan and add the water. Bring to a boil over high heat, then reduce the heat to medium and simmer until tender, about 20 minutes.

While the peels are simmering, prepare the pulp. Trim away and discard about half the pith from the oranges, then quarter them. Quarter the lemons. Cut both the lemon and the orange quarters into lengthwise slices 1/4 inch thick.

Add the orange and lemon slices to the simmering peels. Increase the heat to medium-high and cook, stirring often, for 15 minutes. Remove from the heat and let stand in a cool place for 24 hours.

The next day, return the pan to medium-high heat and add the sugar, stirring to dissolve it. Bring to a gentle boil and cook, stirring often, until the mixture becomes clear, 20 to 30 minutes, then begin to test for the jell point (see instructions on page 22). Alternatively, insert a candy thermometer in the mixture. When it reads 220 degrees F, the marmalade is ready.

Remove from the heat. Skim off and discard any surface foam. Ladle the marmalade into hot, dry, sterilized jars, filling to within 1/2 inch of the rims. Seal with a 1/8-inch-thick layer of melted paraffin (see directions for working with paraffin on page 22). Allow that layer to harden, then add a second layer of the same thickness. Using a damp cloth, wipe the rims clean. Cover with lids, aluminum foil, or with waxed paper or cotton cloth tightly fastened with twine or a rubber band.

Store in a cool, dark place. The marmalade will keep for up to 1 year.

Makes about 4 1/2 pints

# Rose Hip Jelly

FROM THE GATHERING OF THE ROSE HIPS AND THE APPLES TO THE PLOP, PLOP OF THE JUICE DRIPPING THROUGH THE BAG, I AM FASCINATED BY THE PROCESS OF MAKING THIS JELLY BECAUSE IT IS SO BASIC AND CLOSE TO NATURE. FIRST I HARVEST THE LARGE, PLUMP RED-ORANGE ROSE HIPS FROM THE THORNY ROSA RUGOSA BUSHES THAT LINE MY ROAD. NEXT, I GO TO THE CELLAR AND BRING UP SOME OF THE TART GRANNY SMITH APPLES STORED THERE IN LATE OCTOBER. THE APPLES CONTAIN THE PECTIN NECESSARY FOR JELLING.

◆

8 to 10 tart green apples,
such as Granny Smith
1 pound rose hips (about 8 cups),
cut in half
2 quarts water
2 cups granulated sugar

◆

Coarsely chop the apples, including the cores and the seeds. Place in a saucepan with the rose hips and water and bring to a boil over high heat. Reduce the heat to medium-low and simmer until the apples are soft, 20 to 25 minutes. Remove from the heat.

Position a sieve over a container large enough to catch the drippings as they fall through the sieve. Pour the apple mixture into the sieve. With a pestle or the back of a wooden spoon, press against the pieces of apple and rose hip, pushing the resulting pulp through the holes of the sieve. Continue mashing until only skins and seeds remain in the sieve.

Rinse a jelly bag with water, wring it out well, and hang the bag over a large bowl. Transfer the pulpy sieved contents of the bowl to the bag. Leave it to drip. This is a slow process, and one that cannot be hurried!

After an hour or two, the juice will have dripped through. Put this juice in a nonreactive saucepan, add the sugar and, while stirring, bring it to a rolling boil over high heat. Reduce the heat slightly to a gentle boil and cook for approximately 20 minutes, then test for the jell point (see instructions on page 22). Alternatively, insert a candy thermometer in the mixture. When it reads 220 degrees F, the jelly is ready.

Remove from the heat. Skim off and discard any surface foam. Ladle the jelly into hot, dry, sterilized jars, filling to within ¼ inch of the rims. Seal with a ⅛-inch-thick layer of melted paraffin (see directions for working with paraffin on page 22). Allow that layer to harden, then add a second layer of the same thickness. Using a damp cloth, wipe the rims clean. Cover with a lid, aluminum foil, or with waxed paper or cotton cloth tightly fastened with twine or a rubber band.

Store in a cool, dark place. The jelly will keep for up to 1 year.

Makes 2 half-pints

# Candied Grapefruit Peel

*I*n this winter classic, grapefruit slices imbibe sugar syrup until they are saturated. In the process the slices turn from palest pink to amber-rose, while the color of the skin changes from yellow to reddish orange. Once the peels are rolled in sugar, they are a treat worthy of being served at the Christmas party scene in The Nutcracker. It is intriguing to watch the peels metamorphose from sour, pithy trimmings into delectable Victorian candies.

The amount of sugar in this recipe makes a relatively soft peel. If you want a firmer candied peel, use 2 cups sugar to make the syrup.

✦

*2 large grapefruits,*
*Ruby or other variety*
*3 quarts plus 2 cups water*
*1½ cups granulated sugar*

✦

Cut a thin slice from the top and the bottom of each grapefruit. From the top to the bottom, cut through the outer skin and thick whitish pith to the fruit inside, spacing the cuts abut 1 inch apart. Peel the grape-fruits, keeping the skin and pith together.

Cut each of the peel sections lengthwise into long strips ¼ inch wide. You will have about 3 cups. Reserve the fruit for another use.

Pour the 3 quarts water into a saucepan and add the peel strips. Bring the water to a boil over high heat, then reduce the heat to medium. Cook, uncov-ered, until only an inch or so of water remains in the pan, about 1 hour. Using a slotted utensil, remove the peels from the pan and set them aside in a bowl.

In a stainless-steel or other nonreactive sauce-pan, combine the 2 cups water with 1 cup of the sugar. Bring to a boil over high heat, stirring until the sugar dissolves.

Remove from the heat and stir the still-warm peels into the syrup. Let the peels stand for 6 or 7 hours at room tempera-ture. Return the pan to low heat and cook the peels until they have absorbed all of the syrup, about 30 minutes. The peels will become translucent and amber. During the last stages of cooking, keep a close eye on the peels to prevent scorching or burning.

Remove the cooked peels from the pan and spread them in a single layer on a piece of aluminum foil or waxed paper. They will be very sticky and supple. Let the peels stand for about 12 hours to dry slightly.

The next day, roll the peels, one by one, in the remaining ½ cup sugar. Leave them at room temperature for 2 to 3 hours to dry. Pack the candied peels into covered tins, boxes, or glass jars in layers separated by waxed paper. Store in a cool, dry place. The peels will keep for up to 2 months.

Makes about 3 dozen pieces

# Lemon Curd

*L*EMON CURD IS AN OPAQUE EGG-
BASED LEMON CUSTARD MOST OFTEN USED AS A
PIE OR TART FILLING. IT IS ALSO GOOD SPREAD ON
WARM SCONES AND OTHER TEA BREADS.

◆

*6 egg yolks*

*1 cup superfine sugar*

*³/₄ cup fresh lemon juice,
strained (about 5 lemons)*

*Finely grated zest of 4 lemons*

*¹/₂ cup unsalted butter,
cut into ¹/₂-inch cubes*

◆

Combine the egg yolks and sugar in the top pan of a double boiler. Heat the water in the lower pan to a simmer; it must not boil. Using a whisk beat the yolks and sugar together until the mixture becomes creamy and pale and forms thin strands when dropped from the edge of a spoon, about 4 minutes.

Beat in the lemon juice and zest, then gradually stir in the cubes of butter. Continue to cook, stirring constantly, until the mixture is quite thick, about 20 minutes. Be careful not to let the mixture boil, as the eggs will curdle.

Spoon the hot, thickened curd into hot, dry, sterilized jars and cover with tight-fitting lids. Store unopened in the refrigerator for up to 1 month. Once opened the lemon curd will keep for up to 1 week.

Makes 2 pints

# Confit of Roasted Onions

THIN SHAVINGS OF WHITE WINTER ONIONS COOK DOWN TO A THICK MARMALADE CONSISTENCY WHEN ROASTED IN THE OVEN WITH BUTTER, OLIVE OIL, AND HERBS. THE RESULTING CONFIT MAKES A RUSTIC FARMHOUSE-STYLE SPREAD FOR SANDWICHES OR A GLAZE FOR OTHER VEGETABLES OR MEATS.

❖

*4 pounds large white onions*

*¹/₄ cup butter*

*¹/₄ cup olive oil*

*1 teaspoon salt*

*1 teaspoon granulated sugar*

*4 fresh or dried bay leaves*

*2 tablespoons*

*chopped fresh thyme leaves*

❖

Preheat an oven to 350 degrees F.

Cut the onions from top to bottom into slices ¼-inch thick. Using the butter, generously grease a baking sheet that is just large enough to hold the sliced onions in a layer 1 inch deep. Add the onions and sprinkle them with the olive oil, salt, sugar, bay leaves, and thyme.

Place the onions in the preheated oven and roast, turning often, until soft and deep golden brown, 45 minutes to 1 hour. Remove from the oven and let cool to room temperature.

Discard the bay leaves. Pack the onions into dry, sterilized jars with lids. Store in the refrigerator. The onions will keep for up to 2 weeks.

Makes about 3 half-pints

# Ancho Chili Sauce

ELICIOUSLY THICK, DARK, AND SLIGHTLY SMOKY, THIS SAUCE IS PARTICU-
LARLY GOOD WITH SHARP, SOMEWHAT SOUR FRESH CHEESES SUCH AS GOAT CHEESES. IT IS
EQUALLY GOOD WITH PORK, BEEF, OR CHICKEN AND WITH GRILLED OR ROASTED VEGETABLES.
OR USE THIS CLASSIC SALSA FOR DIPPING WARM TORTILLAS OR CRISP CORN CHIPS.

◆

*3 dried ancho chili peppers*

*1 tablespoon water,*

*boiling, or as needed*

*3 tablespoons*

*chopped fresh cilantro*

*1/4 cup well-drained*

*canned plum tomatoes*

*3 fresh tomatillos, husks removed,*

*or well-drained canned tomatillos*

*1/4 teaspoon salt*

*1/4 cup safflower*

*or other vegetable oil*

◆

On a griddle or in a dry frying pan over medium heat, place the chilies. Toast lightly on both sides to bring out the flavor of the chilies and to soften the skin. Remove from the griddle or pan and, when cool enough to handle, remove and discard the stems, seeds, and ribs.

Place the chilies in a blender along with 1 tablespoon boiling water and the cilantro. Process to form a thick paste. Add more water if the mixture seems too dry to form a paste. Add the tomatoes, tomatillos, and salt and continue to process until the mixture is very smooth.

In a frying pan over low heat, warm the oil. Add the chile mixture and cook until the mixture thickens, 4 or 5 minutes. Remove from the heat and let cool to room temperature.

Spoon the sauce into a dry, sterilized jar and cover with a tight-fitting lid. Store in the refrigerator for up to 5 days.

Makes ½ pint

# Pickled Garlic Cloves

*M*ELLOWED BY RED WINE VINEGAR AND AROMATIC HERBS, THE SHARP BITE OF RAW GARLIC IS DIFFUSED. THE PICKLED CLOVES ARE A FINE ADDITION TO SALAD DRESSING OR TO ANY DISH THAT CALLS FOR GARLIC.

❖

*1 cup peeled garlic cloves*

*(about 6 large heads)*

*2 fresh or dried bay leaves*

*1 teaspoon black peppercorns*

*1 teaspoon allspice berries*

*2 or 3 juniper berries*

*$^1/_2$ to $^3/_4$ cup red wine vinegar*

❖

Put the garlic cloves in a dry, sterilized jar with a lid. Add the bay leaves, peppercorns, allspice, and juniper berries to the jar and pour in enough vinegar to cover the cloves. Cover with the lid.

Store in the refrigerator. The garlic will keep for up to 4 months.

Makes ½ pint

# Pickled Whole Onions

*M*Y BEST MEMORIES OF THESE PICKLED, BITE-SIZE ONIONS ARE AS AN ESSEN-TIAL COMPONENT OF THE PLOUGHMAN'S LUNCH, THE SIMPLE COLD PLATE SERVED IN PUBS ALL OVER ENGLAND. A WEDGE OF STILTON CHEESE, SLICES OF DARK BREAD, A BIG SPOONFUL OF CHUTNEY, AND A PINT OF THICK, ROBUST BEER COMPLETE THE MEAL.

◆

*1 pound boiling onions, about*

*1½ inches in diameter*

*3 cups water*

*1 tablespoon salt*

*1 teaspoon mace berries*

*1 teaspoon allspice berries*

*1 teaspoon whole cloves*

*2 cinnamon sticks,*

*each about 4 inches long*

*6 black peppercorns*

*3 cups cider vinegar*

◆

Remove the skin from each onion, trimming but not cutting off the root cluster at the bottom; the root helps keep the onion intact. In a glass bowl, mix together 2 cups of the water and the salt to make a brine. Add the peeled onions and let stand for 24 hours at room temperature.

The next day, cut out an 8-inch square of cheesecloth. Place in the center the mace and allspice berries, cloves, cinnamon sticks, and peppercorns. Gather up the corners and tie them with kitchen string to make a spice bag.

In a stainless-steel or other nonreactive saucepan bring the vinegar and the remaining cup water to a boil over high heat. Add the spice bag, reduce the heat to medium-low, and simmer for 20 minutes. Discard the spice bag and add the onions. Raise the heat and bring back to a boil, then remove from the heat.

Pack the onions into hot, clean, dry sealable jars with lids. Ladle in the hot vinegar mixture, filling to within ½ inch of the rims. Using a damp cloth, wipe the rims clean. Cover with the lids and process for 40 minutes in a hot-water bath (see instructions for processing hot-pack foods on page 21).

Remove the jars and let them cool for 12 hours or overnight. Check for complete seals.

Store the sealed jars in a cool, dark place. The pickled onions will keep for up to 1 year. Once opened, keep them refrigerated. Store any jar lacking a good seal in the refrigerator for up to 2 weeks.

Makes about 2 pints

# Pink Pickled Shallots

*T*HE THIN SHALLOT SLICES TAKE ON A ROSY HUE AFTER SOAKING IN THE RED WINE VINEGAR. THE FINISHED PICKLES CAN BE USED TO MAKE TASTY SPOTS OF COLOR IN SALADS OF ALL KINDS, AND LIKE MANY OTHER TYPES OF PICKLES, GO WELL WITH PLAIN MEATS, BOILED OR ROASTED. CATHERINE BRANDEL, A CHEF AT THE FAMED CHEZ PANISSE IN BERKELEY, CALIFORNIA, SHARED THIS RECIPE WITH ME, WHICH SHE OFTEN PREPARES AT HOME AND AT THE RESTAURANT.

◆

*3/4 pound firm, fresh shallots*

*3/4 cup red wine vinegar*

*1/4 cup granulated sugar*

*1/2 cup water*

*1 fresh or dried bay leaf, bruised*

*3 or 4 fresh thyme sprigs, bruised*

◆

Cut the shallots lengthwise or crosswise into thin slices. Set aside.

In a small stainless-steel or other nonreactive saucepan, combine the vinegar, sugar, water, bay leaf, and thyme. Bring to a boil over high heat. Reduce the heat to medium and simmer for 2 to 3 minutes. Remove from the heat and let cool.

Using a slotted utensil, pack the shallots into dry, sterilized jars with lids. Ladle in the vinegar mixture, filling the jars to within ½ inch of the rims. Cover with the lids.

Store the shallots in the refrigerator for up to 3 weeks.

Makes about 2 half-pints

From left to right:
Pickled Whole Onions
Vin d'Orange
Spicy Lemon Oil
Pickled Garlic Cloves
Pink Pickled Shallots
Pickled Carrots
and Jalapeño Chilies
Confit of Roasted Onions

# Pickled Carrots and Jalapeño Chilies

*T*ART, SHARP, AND SPICY, THESE PICKLED CARROTS AND CHILIES PROVIDE JUST THE RIGHT COUNTERPOINT TO RICH-TASTING FOODS. I LIKE TO STACK THESE PICKLES INSIDE A BIG BARBECUED BEEF SANDWICH, DRIPPING WITH SAUCE, OR FOLD A CARROT OR TWO INTO A FRESHLY STEAMED CORN TORTILLA, ON TOP OF CARNE ASADA AND CILANTRO, THEN ADD A LITTLE SALSA.

✦

*4 large carrots (about 2 pounds)*

*1 large white onion*

*2 fresh jalapeño chili peppers*

*1³/₄ cups water*

*2 teaspoons salt*

*³/₄ cup distilled white vinegar*

*6 black peppercorns*

✦

Cut the carrots on the diagonal into slices about ³/₈ inch thick. Cut the onion crosswise into slices ¼ inch thick. Slice the chili peppers lengthwise into quarters, remove and discard the stems and seeds.

Put the water and salt in a stainless-steel or other nonreactive saucepan and bring to a boil over high heat. Add the carrots, onion, and chilies and lower the heat to medium. Cook for 4 to 5 minutes. The color of the carrots will become brighter and the onions will become almost transparent. Remove from the heat and mix in the vinegar and peppercorns. Let stand for 12 hours or overnight at room temperature.

The next day, using a slotted utensil, pack the carrots, onions, and chili peppers into dry, sterilized jars with lids. Ladle in the vinegar mixture, filling the jars to within ½ inch of the rims. Cover with the lids. Store in the refrigerator for up to several weeks.

Makes about 2 pints

# Whole Preserved Lemons

*I* WAS QUITE THRILLED WHEN I LEARNED HOW TO MAKE THESE LEMONS, BE-
CAUSE THEY HAD ALWAYS SEEMED VERY EXOTIC TO ME. I FIRST SAW THEM—LARGE JARFULS
OF THEM—ON THE COUNTER OF A MIDDLE EASTERN DELICATESSEN IN NEW YORK CITY.
SEVERAL PEOPLE BOUGHT LEMONS WHILE I WAS THERE. THEY PURCHASED TWO OR THREE AT
A TIME, AND THE CLERK DIPPED LONG-HANDLED TONGS INTO THE BIG JARS TO REMOVE THE
FRUITS. I HAD NO IDEA HOW THE LEMONS MIGHT BE USED. LATER, I DISCOVERED THEY WERE
AN IMPORTANT INGREDIENT IN MIDDLE EASTERN SOUPS AND STEWS, WHERE THEY IMPART A
TART, SALTY FLAVOR. I LIKE TO CUT THEM INTO SMALL PIECES AND ADD THEM TO RICH SAL-
ADS MADE WITH DUCK, FOR EXAMPLE, OR SERVE THEM AS AN APPETIZER ALONG WITH OLIVES
AND SALTED NUTS.

DURING PICKLING, THE LEMONS ABSORB SALT FROM THE BRINE AND ARE
FAINTLY FLAVORED BY SPICES. THEY NEED TO SIT FOR ABOUT TWO MONTHS
TO BECOME INFUSED WITH THE SEASONINGS BEFORE EATING.

◆

4½ quarts water

7–10 not-overly ripe lemons

⅔ cup sea salt

2 cinnamon sticks,
each about 3 inches long

4 teaspoons coriander seeds

2 teaspoons black peppercorns

8 whole cloves

1 cup olive oil

◆

Pour 3 quarts of the water into a stainless-steel or other nonreactive saucepan. Bring to a boil over high heat and add the lemons. When the water returns to a boil, cook the lemons for 3 to 4 minutes. Drain and immerse the lemons in cold water until they are cool enough to handle. Drain again and set aside.

While the lemons are cooling, prepare the brine. In a saucepan combine the remaining 1½ quarts water and the salt, cinnamon, coriander seeds, peppercorns, and cloves. Bring the mixture to a boil over high heat and then remove from the heat.

Tightly pack the whole lemons into hot, dry, sterilized jars with lids. If you wish, you can halve or quarter the lemons lengthwise to achieve a tighter fit.

Ladle in the hot brine, including the spices, to within ½ inch of the rims. Add the olive oil and cover with the lids.

Store in a cool, dark place. Let stand for 2 months before using, to allow the lemons to take on the flavors of the brine. The lemons will keep for up to 6 months. Once opened, store in the refrigerator.

Makes 2 quarts

# Spicy Lemon Oil

*I*N THE LITTLE ADRIATIC TOWN OF CHIOGGIA IN NORTHERN ITALY, I ONCE HAD AN EXTREMELY SIMPLE AND WONDERFUL MEAL. THIS OIL REMINDS ME OF IT.

IT WAS IN FEBRUARY IN THE HEART OF WINTER AND LITTLE FRESH PRODUCE WAS AVAILABLE. THE SMALL FAMILY RESTAURANT WHERE WE ATE HAD NEVERTHELESS MADE A BEAUTIFUL DISPLAY OF THE REGION'S SPECIALTY, RADICCHIO, AND OF LEMONS. NEXT TO THEM SAT LARGE GLASS BOWLS, EACH HOLDING A SHALLOW LAYER OF DARK, GOLDEN GREEN OLIVE OIL SPRINKLED WITH CHOPPED PARSLEY.

WHEN OUR DINNER OF FRIED FISH ARRIVED, IT WAS ACCOMPANIED ONLY WITH A PLATE OF THE BRILLIANT RED-AND-WHITE RADICCHIO LEAVES, ONE OF THE BOWLS OF PARSLEY-TOPPED OLIVE OIL, AND SEVERAL HALVED LEMONS. WE WERE INSTRUCTED BY OUR HOST TO SQUEEZE THE LEMON INTO THE OLIVE OIL, TO ADD A LITTLE SALT AND PEPPER, AND TASTE, ADJUSTING AS NECESSARY. WHEN THE VINAIGRETTE WAS DONE TO OUR SATISFACTION, WE HELPED OURSELVES TO THE RADICCHIO, ADDING IT TO THE BOWL WITH THE VINAIGRETTE AND THEN TOSSING IT WELL.

THIS SPICY OIL CAN BE USED FOR SALAD DRESSINGS, COMPLEMENTS BOILED POTATOES, SAUTÉED CHARD, AND OTHER GREEN VEGETABLES, AND IS GOOD FOR DIPPING BREAD.

---

◆

*2 pounds lemons*

*2 tablespoons coriander seeds*

*1 tablespoon black peppercorns*

*6 fresh lemon leaves*

*3 fresh or dried bay leaves*

*4 cups good-quality, fruity olive oil*

◆

Cut each lemon into quarters. Put one third of the cut lemons into a dry, sterilized jar with a lid. Sprinkle with about one third of the coriander seeds and peppercorns, 2 lemon leaves, and 1 bay leaf. Repeat the layers twice, then cover with the lid. Let stand for 24 hours in a cool place.

The next day, pour the olive oil into the jar and cover it again. Let stand for 3 days.

At the end of 3 days, remove and discard the lemons. Strain the oil through a sieve lined with several layers of cheesecloth. Decant into a dry, sterilized bottle. Seal with a cork and store the bottle in a cool, dark place. The oil will keep for up to 1 month.

Makes 1 quart

## Vin d'Orange

THIS IS A CALIFORNIA VERSION OF
AN OLD FRENCH FARMHOUSE RECIPE FOR A
FLAVORED, FORTIFIED WINE. PEELS FROM EATEN
ORANGES ARE SAVED AND DRIED, THEN TOASTED
IN THE OVEN, FROM WHERE THEY FILL THE HOUSE
WITH AN INTENSE AROMA OF ORANGE OILS.
ALCOHOL, IN THIS CASE VODKA, AND SUGAR ARE
ADDED, ALONG WITH THE ORANGE PEELS, TO A
DRY, ROBUST RED WINE SUCH AS A CALIFORNIA
ZINFANDEL. THE FLAVORED WINE SHOULD REST IN
A COOL, DARK PLACE FOR AT LEAST A MONTH, BUT
THE FLAVORS IMPROVE THE LONGER IT STANDS.

IN MY OPINION, THE PERFECT MOMENT FOR
SERVING A VIN D'ORANGE À LA MAISON APERITIF
WINE IS ON WARM SUMMER NIGHTS, SITTING
OUTSIDE WITH FRIENDS.

◆

*Dried peels of 6 small
or 4 large oranges
1 fifth dry red wine,
such as Zinfandel
3/4 cup granulated sugar
1/2 cup vodka*

◆

Preheat an oven to 300 degrees F.

Spread the orange peels on a baking sheet. Place in the preheated oven and toast, turning from time to time, until the inner white portion of the peels is golden and the outer skin has deepened to dark orange. This toasting process, which takes about 45 minutes, gives a rich caramel undertone to the wine.

Place the wine, sugar, vodka, and toasted peels in a dry, sterilized widemouthed jar with a lid. Cover with the lid. Store the jar in a cool, dark place, turning it upside down several times a day for a week until the sugar dissolves, then store for at least 1 month but preferably 2 or 3 months.

At this time, strain the wine through a fine-mesh sieve; discard the peels. Decant into dry, sterilized wine or other attractive glass bottles. Cork them and store in a cool, dark place. The wine will keep for up to 1 year.

Makes about 1 quart

## Cayenne Walnuts

$\mathcal{E}$NCRUSTED WITH A SPARKLING COAT OF CAYENNE PEPPER, SUGAR, SALT, AND GINGER AND THEN SLOWLY TOASTED IN AN OVEN, THESE SPICY MORSELS REQUIRE LITTLE TIME OR EXPERTISE TO MAKE. THEY ARE SAVORY ADDITIONS TO BOTH GREEN AND FRUIT SALADS— IF THEY AREN'T EATEN OUT OF HAND FIRST.

✦

2 tablespoons cayenne pepper

1½ teaspoons granulated sugar

1½ teaspoon salt

¾ teaspoon ground ginger

6 egg whites

3 cups walnut halves
(about ¾ pound)

✦

Preheat an oven to 225 degrees F.

In a small bowl stir together the cayenne pepper, sugar, salt, and ginger. Place the egg whites in another bowl and, using a whisk or fork, beat until frothy but not stiff. Using a small paint brush or your fingertips, lightly brush each walnut half with a small amount of the egg white and then sprinkle it with some of the cayenne mixture. As each walnut half is coated, place it on a baking sheet.

When all of the walnuts are coated, place the baking sheet in the preheated oven until the nuts are toasted and crunchy and the coating is crisp, 15 to 20 minutes.

Remove from the oven and let the nuts cool completely. Pack the spiced nuts into a covered tin, box, or glass jar. Store in a dry place.

The nuts will keep for up to 3 months.

Makes 3 cups

*Salted Blanched Almonds*

R AW NATURAL ALMONDS ARE FIRST BRIEFLY SOAKED IN BOILING WATER, AND
THEN THE THIN, PAPERY HUSKS ARE SLIPPED OFF, LEAVING THE GLEAMING, PURE IVORY NUTS
UNADORNED. AFTER BEING ROLLED IN A LITTLE SALT, THE IVORY TONES GLITTER. THE
FRESHER THE ALMONDS, THE MORE EASILY THE HUSKS WILL SLIP OFF.

◆

*4 cups almonds*

*(about 1 pound)*

*8 cups water, boiling*

*4 egg whites*

*1 cup fine salt*

◆

Put the almonds in a bowl and pour the boiling water over them. Let stand for 1 minute, then drain. Using your fingers, gently rub the brown skins until they slip off the nuts. If the skins don't slip off easily, once again pour boiling water over the nuts. This time, let the nuts stand only 30 seconds, just long enough to loosen the skins, then drain and skin.

Place the egg whites in a small bowl and, using a whisk or fork, beat until frothy but not stiff. Using a small paint brush or your fingertips, lightly brush a little of the egg white on each almond and then sprinkle with salt. If you use too much egg white, the salt will adhere thickly, making for a very salty—perhaps too salty—nut. As the nuts are salted, place them in a single layer on waxed paper and let dry for several hours or overnight.

Store in covered tins, boxes, or glass jars in a cool, dry place. The nuts will keep for 2 to 3 months.

Makes 4 cups

## ACKNOWLEDGMENTS

*There are numerous people behind the words, the thoughts, and the photographs that make this book more than the sum of its parts. Our heartfelt thanks to them all:*

To Michaele Thunen for her generous help throughout the seasons of this volume. To Jacqueline Jones for her light touch with our work and her beautiful designs. To Kristen Jester for always being at hand when needed. To Michele Miller for her unending support and assistance. To Dimitri Spathis for his assistance. To editor Bill LeBlond at Chronicle Books for his clear vision, creativity, and understanding. To Sharon Silva for her careful and thoughtful editing of the manuscript. To Ed Haverty for his help throughout. To my daughter, Ethel Brennan, for the enthusiasm and professionalism she brought to the task of recipe testing. To my husband, Jim Schrupp, who reads every word I write and eats everything I cook. To Oliver Brennan and Tom and Dan Schrupp who are my most discerning culinary critics. And to Karen Frerichs for her cheerful and professional assistance in recipe testing. A special thanks to my agent, Susan Lescher.

Especially from Kathryn: Deep thanks to my husband, Michael Schwab, and my boys, Eric and Peter, for their love and support.

*For produce, linens, ribbons, and other sundries:*

A special thanks to Bill Fujimoto at Monterey Market in Berkeley. To Stuart Dixon of Stonefree Farms in Davis and Watsonville, for giving us the freedom to roam his fields to collect tomatoes, sweet peppers, herbs, and greens. To Frank Martin and his sister, Madeline Jimenez, fruit growers in Winters, for the cherry-laden branches they gave us, and to Knoll Organic Farms in Brentwood for the purple artichokes they shipped to us when Georgeanne's garden crop had finished. To Anna Le Blanc for giving us rose and lemon clippings from her Berkeley yard whenever we asked, and to Leonard and Nancy Becker who gifted us with oranges on branches. To Susan Kirshenbaum for her beautiful calligraphy on jar labels.

To Betty Jane Roth, of Chico, who loaned us antique linens and kitchen utensils, as did Carla Nasaw of Ross, and in Berkeley, to Mimi Luebbermann who let us use her antique silver flatware and jars and Devorah Nussenbaum who allowed us to delve into her ribbon collection.

*Many of the props that appear in these pages are available at the following stores:*

Ribbons and ornaments:
Tail of the Yak,
Berkeley, California;
Bell'occhio,
San Francisco, California

Antique linens:
Lacis,
Berkeley, California

Garden and tabletop accessories:
The Gardener,
Berkeley, California

Canning jars and accessories:
Sur la Table,
Seattle, Washington

Antique canning jars:
Clementine's,
Chico, California

Antique kitchenware:
Bonnie Grossman,
Ames Gallery,
Berkeley, California

Brennan, Georgeanne,
Isaac Cronin and
Charlotte Glenn.
*The New American
Vegetable Cookbook.*
Reading, Massachusetts:
Aris Books/Addison-
Wesley, 1985.

Carey, Norma. *Perfect
Preserves.* New York:
Stewart, Tabori &
Chang, Inc., 1990.

McGee, Harold. *On
Food and Cooking.* New
York: Scribner's Sons,
1984.

Medecin, Jacques.
*Cuisine du Comté de
Nice.* Paris: Julliard,
1972.

Reboul, J.B. *La
Cuisinière Provençale.*
6th ed., Marseille:
Tacussel, 1985.

Sorzio, Angelo. *Le
Conserve.* Milan: Gruppo
Editoriale Fabbri, 1983.

Time-Life. *Preserving.*
Alexandria,Virginia:
Time-Life Books, 1981.

## TABLE OF EQUIVALENTS

*The exact equivalents in the following tables have been rounded for convenience.*

*Equivalents for Common Ingredients*

### US / UK

oz = ounce
lb = pound
in = inch
ft = foot
tbl = tablespoon
fl oz = fluid ounce
qt = quart

### METRIC

g = gram
kg = kilogram
mm = millimeter
cm = centimeter
ml = milliliter
l = liter

### WEIGHTS

| US / UK | Metric |
| --- | --- |
| 1 oz | 30 g |
| 2 oz | 60 g |
| 3 oz | 90 g |
| 4 oz (¼ lb) | 125 g |
| 5 oz (⅓ lb) | 155 g |
| 6 oz | 185 g |
| 7 oz | 220 g |
| 8 oz (½ lb) | 250 g |
| 10 oz | 315 g |
| 12 oz (¾ lb) | 375 g |
| 14 oz | 440 g |
| 16 oz (1 lb) | 500 g |
| 1½ lb | 750 g |
| 2 lb | 1 kg |
| 3 lb | 1.5 kg |

### OVEN TEMPERATURES

| Fahrenheit | Celsius | Gas |
| --- | --- | --- |
| 250 | 120 | ½ |
| 275 | 140 | 1 |
| 300 | 150 | 2 |
| 325 | 160 | 3 |
| 350 | 180 | 4 |
| 375 | 190 | 5 |
| 400 | 200 | 6 |
| 425 | 220 | 7 |
| 450 | 230 | 8 |
| 475 | 240 | 9 |
| 500 | 260 | 10 |

### LIQUIDS

| US | Metric | UK |
| --- | --- | --- |
| 2 tbl | 30 ml | 1 fl oz |
| ¼ cup | 60 ml | 2 fl oz |
| ⅓ cup | 80 ml | 3 fl oz |
| ½ cup | 125 ml | 4 fl oz |
| ⅔ cup | 160 ml | 5 fl oz |
| ¾ cup | 180 ml | 6 fl oz |
| 1 cup | 250 ml | 8 fl oz |
| 1½ cups | 375 ml | 12 fl oz |
| 2 cups | 500 ml | 16 fl oz |
| 4 cups / 1 qt | 1 l | 32 fl oz |

### BROWN SUGAR

| | | |
| --- | --- | --- |
| ¼ cup | 1½ oz | 45 g |
| ½ cup | 3 oz | 90 g |
| ¾ cup | 4 oz | 125 g |
| 1 cup | 5½ oz | 170 g |
| 1½ cups | 8 oz | 250 g |
| 2 cups | 10 oz | 315 g |

### WHITE SUGAR

| | | |
| --- | --- | --- |
| ¼ cup | 2 oz | 60 g |
| ⅓ cup | 3 oz | 90 g |
| ½ cup | 4 oz | 125 g |
| ¾ cup | 6 oz | 185 g |
| 1 cup | 8 oz | 250 g |
| 1½ cups | 12 oz | 375 g |
| 2 cups | 1 lb | 500 g |

### RAISINS / CURRANTS / SEMOLINA

| | | |
| --- | --- | --- |
| ¼ cup | 1 oz | 30 g |
| ⅓ cup | 2 oz | 60 g |
| ½ cup | 3 oz | 90 g |
| ¾ cup | 4 oz | 25 g |
| 1 cup | 5 oz | 155 g |

### JAM / HONEY

| | | |
| --- | --- | --- |
| 2 tbl | 2 oz | 60 g |
| ¼ cup | 3 oz | 90 g |
| ½ cup | 5 oz | 155 g |
| ¾ cup | 8 oz | 250 g |
| 1 cup | 1 l oz | 345 g |